SoulTou

Creative Awakening

COLORING JOURNAL

Created by
Deborah Koff-Chapin

Find out about Deborah's artwork,
the process of Touch Drawing,
SoulCards and SoulTouch Coloring Journals at
www.touchdrawing.com

Center for Touch Drawing
Resources for Creative Awakening

Langley, Washington USA

ISBN 978-0-9645623-8-7

How to Use SoulTouch™ Coloring Journals

Materials

Art materials are full of creative potential! Use colored pencils, markers, watercolor pencils, brush markers, crayons, oil pastels, and metallic or gel pens. The paper can handle wet mediums like watercolor or acrylic with minimal buckling. Try collage with photographs or colored papers. It's great to have a few mediums available. Combining them on an image can bring richness and depth.

When and Where to Color

The process of coloring will help you shift into another way of being. Use the coloring journal during a break in your workday, in a waiting room, on a plane or while listening to a presentation. It is a great way to slow down before sleeping. If you have the time and space, create a contemplative atmosphere before you color. Turn off your phone and light a candle. Work in silence or listen to relaxing music. Or gather with friends for a coloring circle.

Choosing an Image

Before looking through the images, take a moment to be open. Then browse the pages until you find one that speaks to you. Drink it in with your eyes. Notice the textures, shapes and patterns. As you come into relationship with your selected image, can you imagine colors, movements or forms that you might add to it? Or do words start to come? Begin with whichever modality is moving within you: coloring or writing.

Coloring

This is a safe place to practice trusting your own process. Simply choose a color that calls to you and begin. Bring out the forms you see on the page, add patterns or shapes. Feel free to color over the printed lines, or leave areas of the image untouched. Play with layering colors. Fill in the spaces around the image. You might even add words in a graphic style. Look at the inside back cover of this book to see examples of the different ways people color the same image.

Every now and then, stop coloring and take in what you have done so far. Sometimes it helps to leave it for a while, to view it with fresh eyes when you return. One image might feel complete with a few simple areas of color; another might call you further and further into it, layering and refining until it comes to a new depth and vibrancy.

Be willing to take risks. The expectation of perfection can inhibit creative expression. When you work with mistakes, you open to new and exciting possibilities. If in the end you are not so happy with a particular page, just let it be. You might actually appreciate it more later on. The creative process always has ups and downs. Use your art as a practice. The most vital creative endeavor is your life, not a product on paper.

Writing in this Journal

If you want to keep the book intact, write on the lined page across from the image. If you prefer to take your colored pictures out of the book, write on the back of the page, so words and image remain together. The paper is thick enough that ink won't bleed through onto the image side. It's best to write with a gentle touch. Some pens or pencils might etch impressions into the paper if too much pressure is used.

Writing Process

There are many reflective and creative writing techniques. Here are a few simple suggestions: First of all, simply open your mind, gaze at the image and see if a title comes into your awareness. What begins as a title may grow into a longer poetic statement. You may also ask a question, engaging in imaginary dialogue with the image. Invite it to tell you its story, or give you a message. It is amazing what insights can emerge.

Coloring, Writing & Sharing in a Group

This is a wonderful activity to engage in with friends and family. Children and adults can happily sit together and color these images. If you work in a human service profession, there may be a setting into which you can bring them. It is easy to share one book within a group. Carefully tear the perforated pages out and allow each person to select the one they want to color.

Coloring can be done in an informal and light-hearted manner, along with conversation, music and snacks. If you want a deeper experience, you can guide your group through the steps outlined in these instructions. You might begin by sitting in a circle and checking in, giving each person a couple of minutes to share. When you go into the time of coloring and writing, encourage participants to stay silently with their own process. It is a rare and wonderful thing to spend time with others in a non-verbal way. When you come back together, your communication is enriched through the sharing of images, writing and insights. If you meet regularly, this can develop into a precious creative support group.

What to do with the Images

Fill your book with color and writing, and keep it as a journal. Or take pages out for framing or to use as gifts. You can also photograph your colored images and use them as screen savers, wallpaper for your phone, or post in social media with your writing. Please credit *SoulTouch Coloring Journal*. Go to www.touchdrawing.com to connect with our social media community. If you want to color the same images again, you can purchase an electronic version on the site.

Creating Your Own Touch Drawings

The images in this book were created by Deborah Koff-Chapin through the process of Touch Drawing. Find out more about how you can create your own images through this simple yet deep way of drawing.

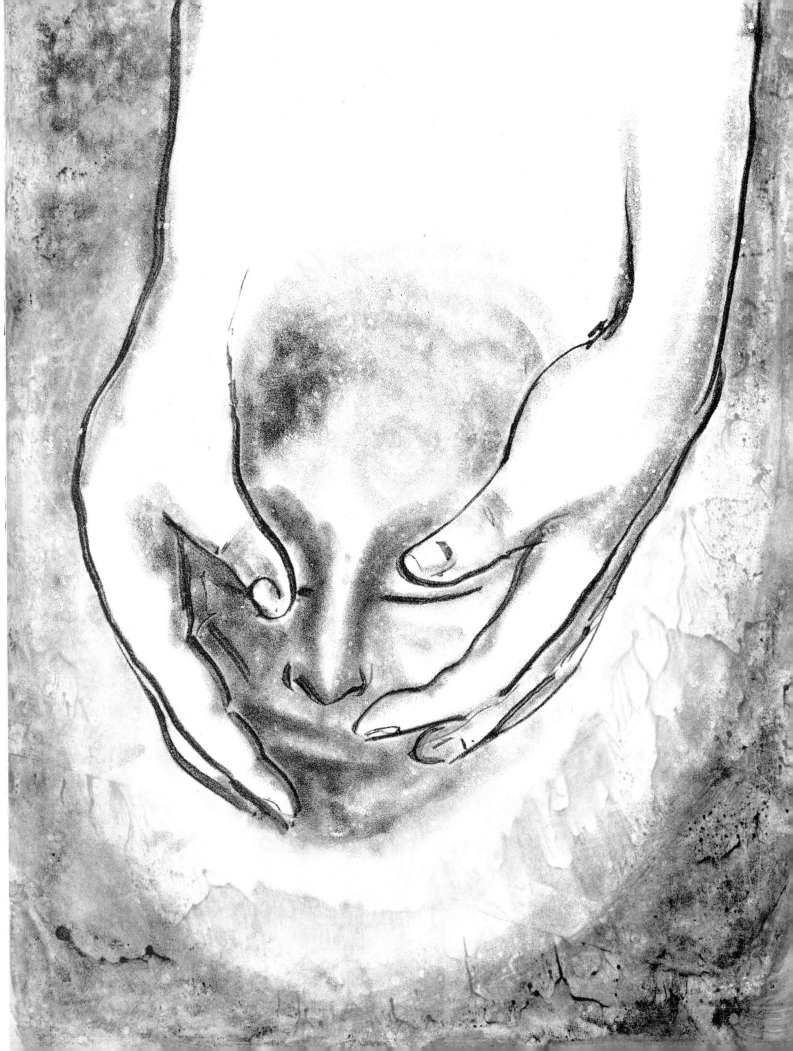

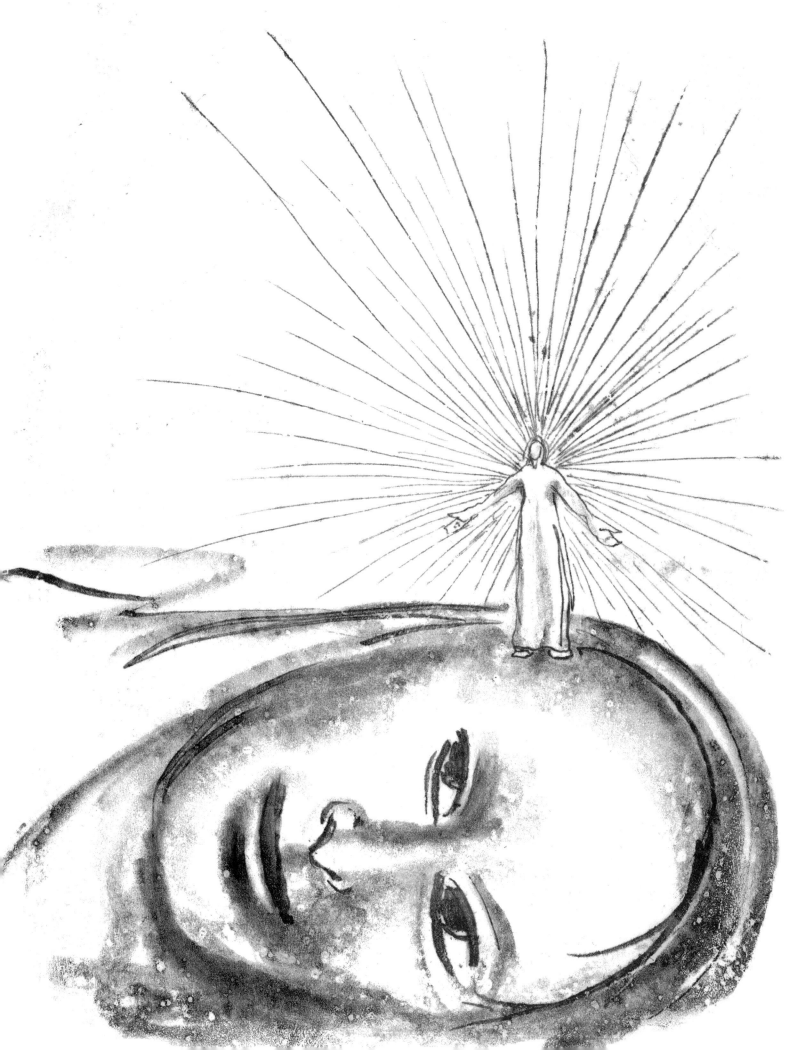

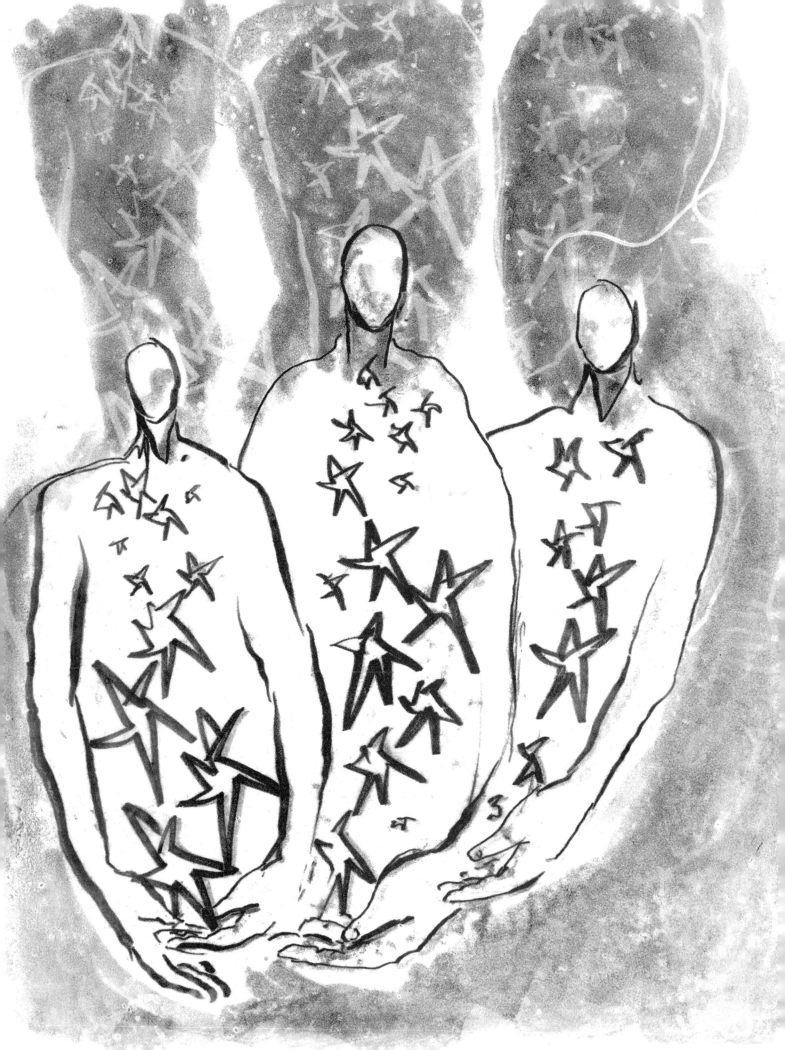

The images in this book have an evocative power that stems from the way in which they were created. They emerged out of 40 years of work with Touch Drawing. In 1974, on my last day in art school, I came upon this simple yet profound process in an ecstatic creative moment. Moving my hands over paper that was laid upon a smooth surface of paint, I lifted it to see the imprint of my touch on the underside. This direct form of expression had a primal, enlivening, power. Over the years I have deepened my practice of Touch Drawing, and introduced the process to people around the world. If you are moved by the images in this journal, you might like to try creating your own through Touch Drawing. It is a deep and transformative experience. The website offers inspiring stories, educational media and art materials so you can begin Touch Drawing on your own or with others.

You can also find out about SoulCards 1 & 2, card decks of my images in full color. Use them to access insight and intuition. The website has free ecards and galleries that share many facets of my work, including Interpretive Touch Drawing and Inner Portraits.

Find out more about SoulTouch Coloring Journals on the site as well. Connect with other colorists through our social media, and read stories of what inspired some of the images in this book. Receive bonus digital downloads to print when you sign the mailing list. All this and more can be found at:

www.touchdrawing.com

I offer my gratitude to the people who played a role in bringing these coloring journals into being: Gretchen Kramph, Diana Stimmel, Jeff Vander Klute and Maria Bäck who provided seminal ideas at pivotal moments; To Steven Wallace at New Leaf whose affirmation and support confirmed this was the right project at the right time. To Vicki Grayson Liden whose graphic skill and enormous focus brought these books into form; To all the friends and colleagues who colored pages - It was so exciting to see my images come alive with your unique approaches! Loving gratitude to my husband Ross Chapin, who has been by my side through it all; And deep thanks to the Spirit of Touch Drawing and all who practice it, for the inspiration and the calling.

—Deborah Koff-Chapin